Note to parents
The **Lifesize Animal Counting Book** is an ideal starting point for children who are just beginning to investigate numbers and how they work. Parents can devise counting games based on the photographs, and non-readers can guess at the words by counting the animals on each page. Children will learn numbers from one to ten, twenty, and one hundred by looking first at numerals, then at words, and the photographs of familiar animals turn learning about numbers into fun!

A DORLING KINDERSLEY BOOK
www.dk.com

Editor Djinn von Noorden
Designer Ingrid Mason
Assistant designer Susan St. Louis
Production Ruth Cobb

First published in Great Britain in 1994 by
Dorling Kindersley Limited
9 Henrietta Street, London WC2E 8PS

A CIP catalogue record for this book is available from the British Library

ISBN 0-7513-5128-8

Colour reproduction by Colourscan, Singapore
Printed in Italy by L.E.G.O.

The Lifesize
Animal Counting Book

DK

DORLING KINDERSLEY
London • New York • Stuttgart

1
one

One greedy gorilla

2
two

Two contented cats

3
three

Three playful puppies

4
four

Four slow tortoises

5
five

14

Five wise owls

6
six

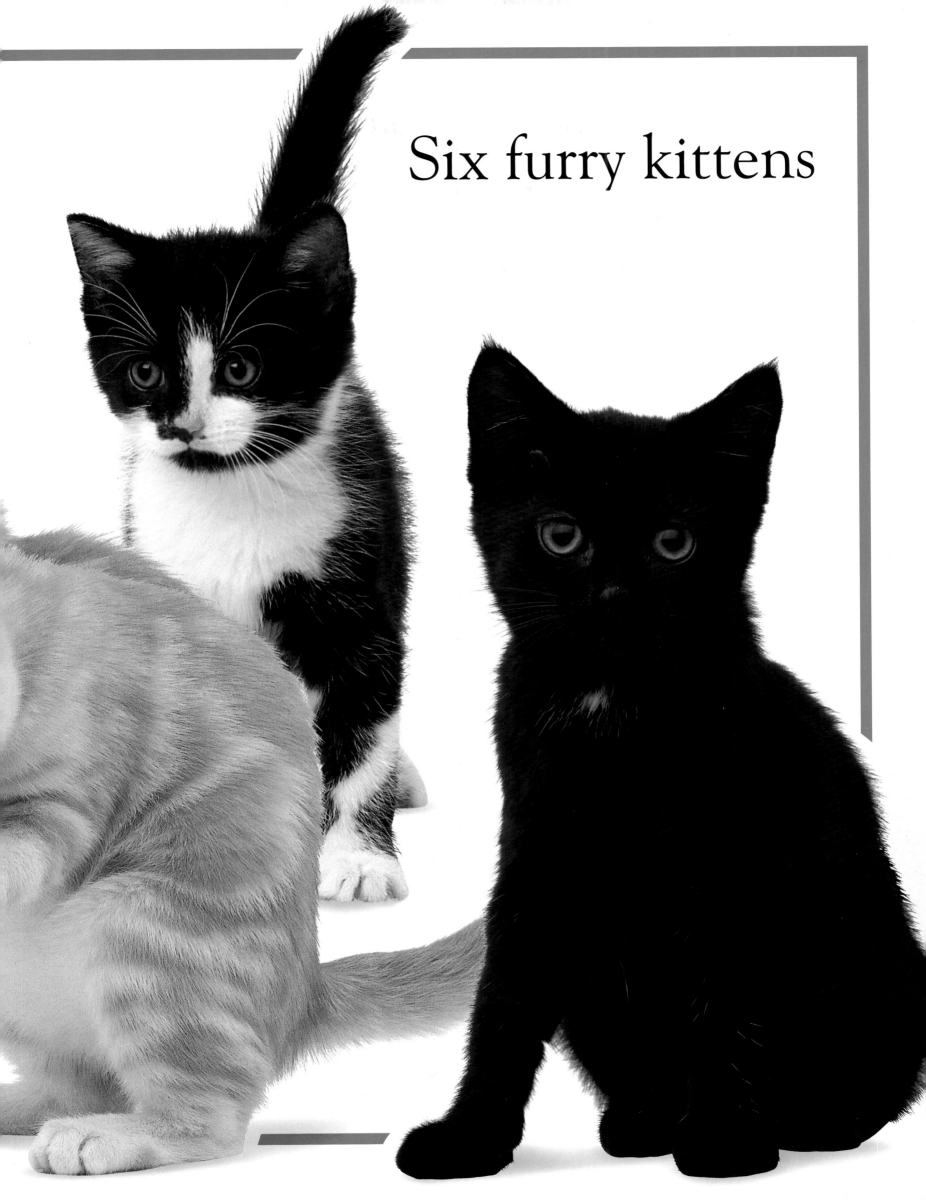

Six furry kittens

7
seven

Seven snuffly rabbits

8
eight

Three white ducks and five
fluffy ducklings
make eight

9
nine

Nine nosey guinea pigs

10
ten

Nine cheeping chicks
and one fat hen
make
ten

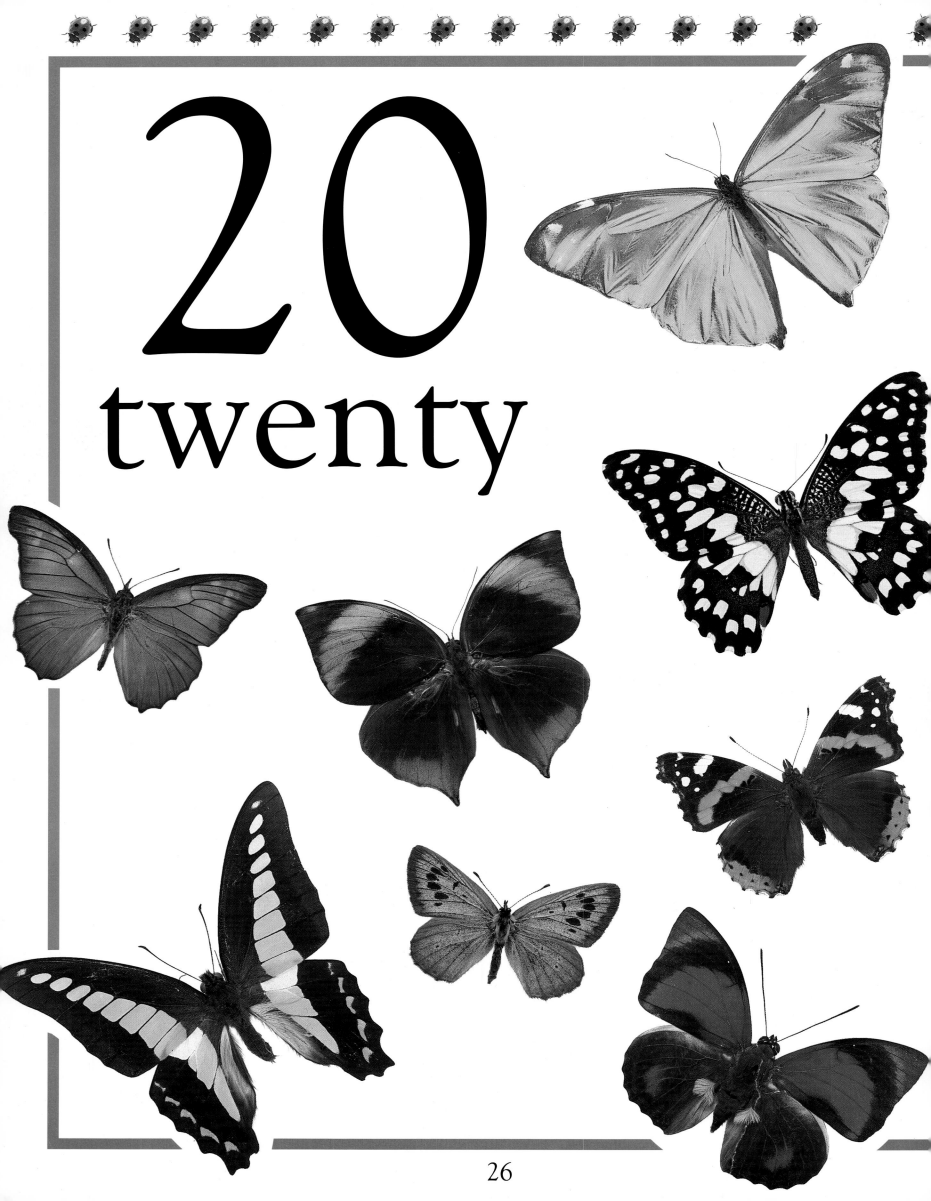

20
twenty

Twenty beautiful
butterflies

100
one hundred

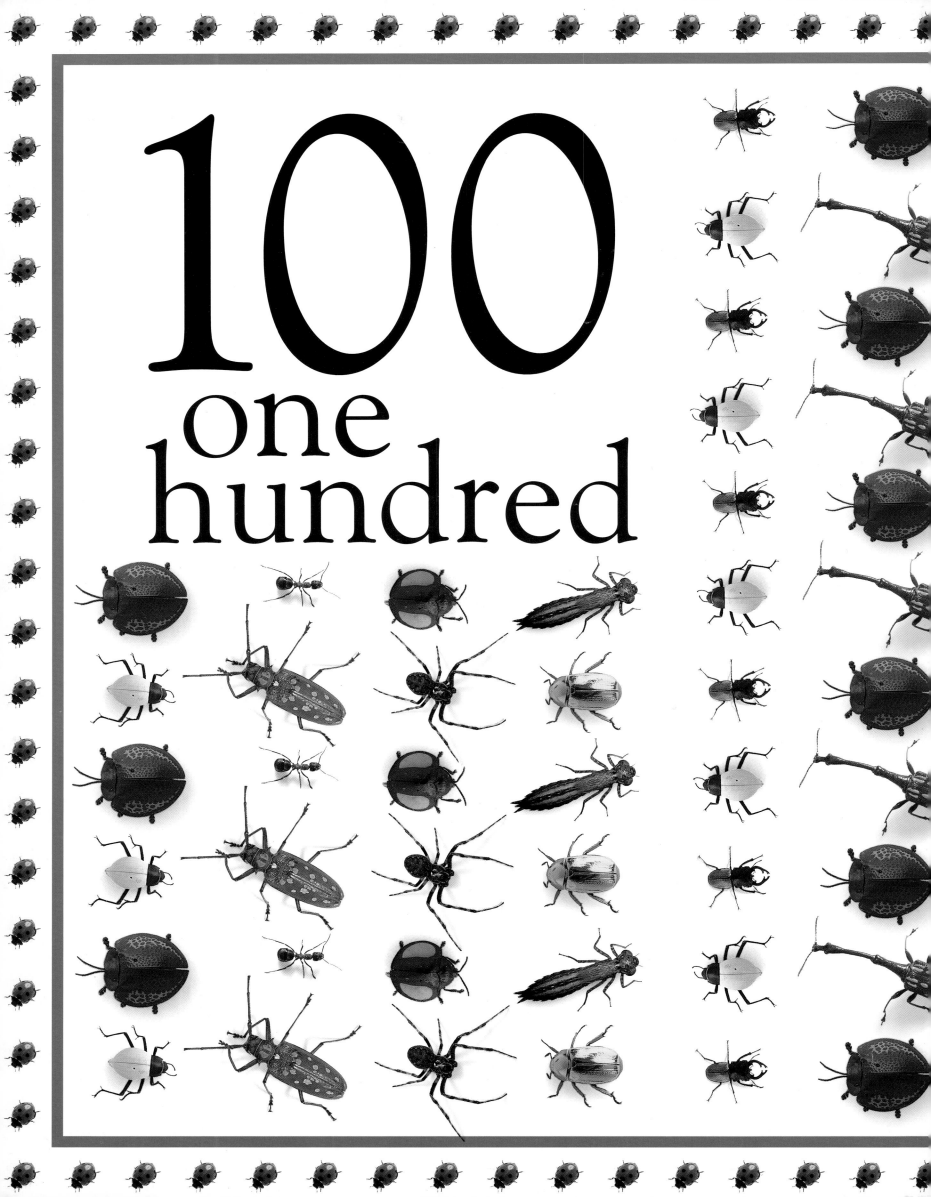

One hundred
creepy crawlies.
How many spiders
can you see?